Reflections

People We Know

Homework and Practice Book

Grade 2

Harcourt

SCHOOL PUBLISHERS

Orlando   Austin   New York   San Diego   Toronto   London

Visit *The Learning Site!*
www.harcourtschool.com

Reflections

The activities in this book reinforce social studies concepts and skills in Harcourt School Publishers' *Reflections: People We Know*. There is one activity for each lesson and skill. In addition to activities, this book also contains reproductions of the graphic organizers that appear in the unit reviews in the Student Edition. Study guides for student review are also provided. Reproductions of the activity pages appear with answers in the Teacher Edition.

Contents

UNIT 3: GOVERNING THE PEOPLE

UNIT 4: USING OUR RESOURCES

UNIT 5: PEOPLE IN THE MARKETPLACE

UNIT 6: PEOPLE MAKE A DIFFERENCE

Name _____ Date _____

Community Changes

Number the pictures to show the correct order of the changes that happen in this community.

Name _____ Date _____

CHART AND GRAPH SKILLS
Read a Calendar

Use Madison's calendar to answer the questions.

June 2008						
S	**M**	**T**	**W**	**T**	**F**	**S**
1	2	3	4	5	6 Last day of school	7
8	9	10	11	12	13	14
		Trip to Grandmother's				
15 Father's Day	16	17	18	19	20 Children's Theater	21
22	23	24	25	26	27	28
29	30 Mother's birthday!					

1 What month is on the calendar? _____

2 How many days are in this month? _____

3 When is the last day of school? _____

4 How many days will Madison visit her grandmother?

_____

5 What day of the week is Madison going to the

Children's Theater? _____

Name ______________________________ Date ____________

Family Events

Make a storyboard of three family events.

Write a sentence about each event.

____

____

____

____

____

____

CALIFORNIA STANDARDS HSS 2.1.3

Name _____ Date _____

CHART AND GRAPH SKILLS
Mark's Summer Vacation

Read the events on the time line. Then write a story about
Mark's summer vacation.

Have a Great Summer!

School ends, May 30

Seventh birthday, July 24

May	June	July	August

Camp begins, June 17

School begins, August 25

Welcome to Grade 2

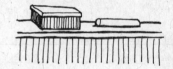

_____

_____

_____

_____

_____

CALIFORNIA STANDARDS HSS 2.1.3; CS 1

Name _____ Date _____

Future Artifact

Draw a picture of an object that could be a future artifact about your life. Finish the sentence to tell why you chose this object.

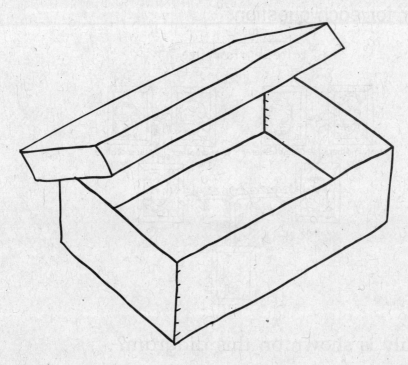

I would choose a _____ as my artifact

because _____

_____

_____

_____

_____

_____

Name _____ Date _____

CHART AND GRAPH SKILLS
Family Tree

Look at the diagram of the family tree. Circle the
correct answer for each question.

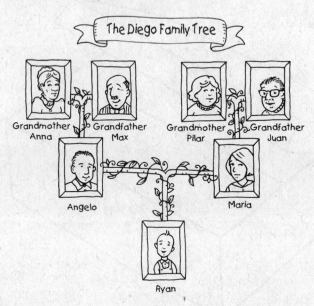

① What family is shown on this diagram?

The Diego Family   **The Lopez Family**

② What is the name of Angelo's father?

Juan   **Max**

③ Who is the youngest person?

Ryan   **Max**

④ Who is Ryan's mother?

Pilar   **Maria**

⑤ How many children do Angelo and Maria have?

1   **2**

CALIFORNIA STANDARDS HSS 2.1.1

6 ■ **Homework and Practice Book**   Use after reading Unit 1, Skill Lesson, pages 42–43.

Name _____ Date _____

Pass on a Tradition!

Draw a picture to show something the person on the
left might pass on to the person on the right.

Name _____ Date _____

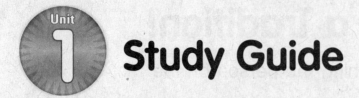

Study Guide

Read the paragraph. Use the words in the Word Bank to fill in the blanks.

ancestors	artifacts	communication	events
history	storyboard	tradition	

_____ is the story of how people and

places change over time. Families have their own stories

about change. Some people put pictures and words on a

_____ to show important _____

in their lives. Other families pass down _____,

or objects from the past. These objects once belonged to their

_____. Sometimes older family members show

younger family members how their family has always done

something. They pass along a _____. People

may also write and tell each other about how their lives

change. Sharing this information is _____.

🐻 CALIFORNIA STANDARDS HSS 2.1, 2.1.1

Name _____ Date _____

Reading Social Studies

Fill in the chart to show the order in which events in Lan's family history happened.

First

Lan's ancestors traveled from Vietnam.

Last

CALIFORNIA STANDARDS HSS 2.1, 2.1.3; ELA 2.2.5

Name _____ Date _____

Where Is That Place?

Look at the map and the map legend. Then follow the directions.

1. Draw a flag on the flagpole next to the school.

2. Color the lake in the park blue.

3. Add another symbol to the empty block on the map. Put your symbol in the map legend, and label your symbol.

CALIFORNIA STANDARDS HSS 2.2, 2.2.2; CS 4

Name _____   Date _____

MAP AND GLOBE SKILLS
Map Grid

Use the map grid to answer the questions.

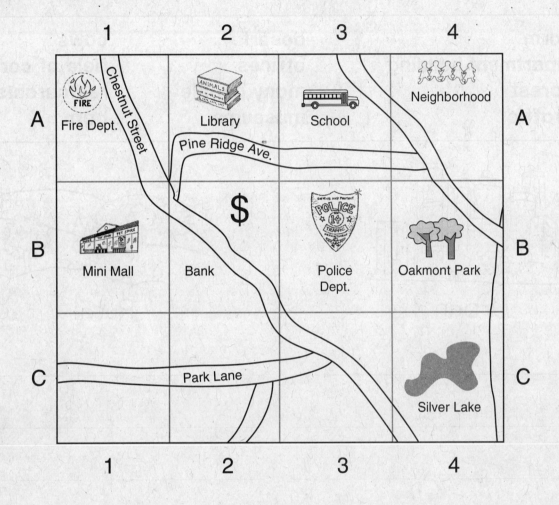

1 In which square is the library? _____

2 What place is in B-3? _____

3 In which square is Silver Lake? _____

Name _____ Date _____

Urban or Rural?

Decide where you would find each item listed in the Word Bank.
Then write it under Urban or Rural.

farm	desert	cows
apartment building	offices	field of corn
forest	many people	restaurants
traffic	museums	barn

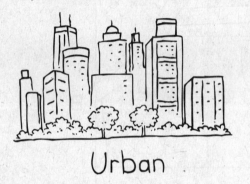

Urban

Rural

_____   _____

_____   _____

_____   _____

_____   _____

_____   _____

CALIFORNIA STANDARDS HSS 2.2.4; HI 2

12 ■ Homework and Practice Book   Use after reading Unit 2, Lesson 2, pages 82–87.

Name _____ Date _____

MAP AND GLOBE SKILLS
How Far?

Look at the map. Use the map scale to help you answer
the questions.

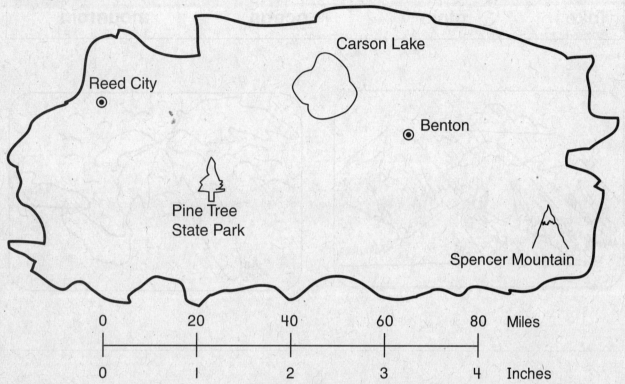

Carson Lake

Reed City
⊙

Benton
⊙

Pine Tree
State Park

Spencer Mountain

| 0 | 20 | 40 | 60 | 80 | Miles |

| 0 | 1 | 2 | 3 | 4 | Inches |

❶ What information does the map scale tell you?

_____

_____

❷ On the map, about how many inches is Reed City from

Carson Lake? _____

❸ About how many miles is Pine Tree State Park from

Benton? _____

CALIFORNIA STANDARDS HSS 2.2.2; CS 4

Identify Land and Water

Use a word from the Word Bank to describe each picture.
Then color the water landforms blue.

| lake | plain | ocean | mountain |

_____

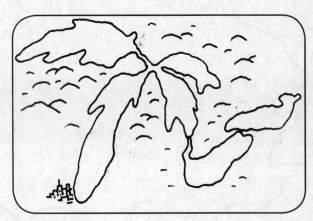

_____

_____

_____

🐻 CALIFORNIA STANDARDS HSS 2.2.2

14 ■ Homework and Practice Book   Use after reading Unit 2, Lesson 3, pages 90–95.

Name _____ Date _____

MAP AND GLOBE SKILLS
Find Places on a Map

Answer the questions about the states shown on the map.

Use the directional indicator to help you.

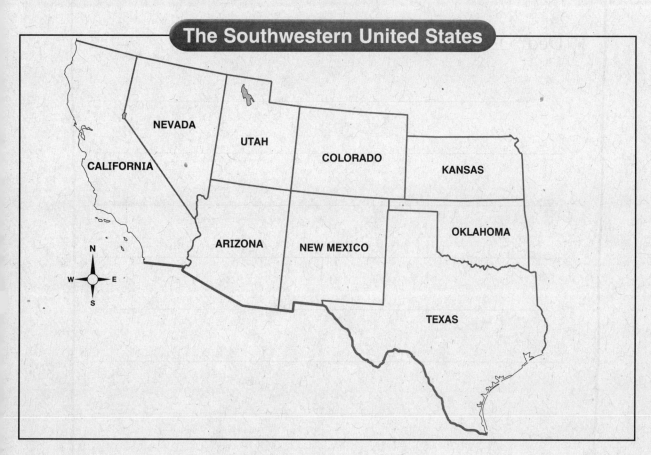

The Southwestern United States

NEVADA

UTAH

COLORADO

KANSAS

CALIFORNIA

ARIZONA

NEW MEXICO

OKLAHOMA

TEXAS

N W E S

1 Which state is north of Arizona? _____

2 Which state is farthest south on the map? _____

3 Which state is farthest west on the map? _____

4 Which state is east of Colorado? _____

5 Which state is north of New Mexico? _____

[bear icon] CALIFORNIA STANDARDS HSS 2.2, 2.2.2; CS 4

Name _____ Date _____

Letter from Far Away

Pretend you are an immigrant in the United States. Write a letter home, telling about your trip and your life in the United States.

Dear _____ ,

_____

_____

_____

_____

_____

_____

_____

_____

Yours truly,

_____

CALIFORNIA STANDARDS HSS 2.2.3

16 ■ Homework and Practice Book Use after reading Unit 2, Lesson 4, pages 100–105.

Name _____ Date _____

MAP AND GLOBE SKILLS
The Sheriff's Busy Day

Read the story. Draw the route on the map, and answer the question.

The sheriff of Cowtown is going to pick up some feed for his horse. First, he stops to buy a new shirt at the dry goods store. Next, he checks the railroad station to see if anyone new has just come in on the train. Then, he goes to the bank to get some more money. Finally, he arrives at the feed store.

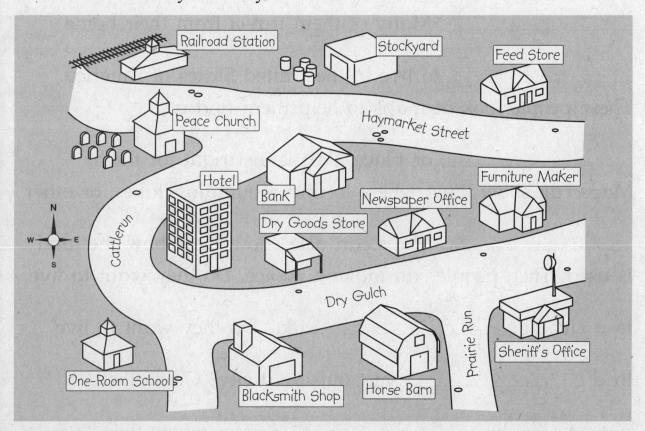

Which streets does the sheriff take to get to the feed store?

_____

CALIFORNIA STANDARDS HSS 2.2, 2.2.2; CS 4

Name _____ Date _____

Study Guide

Read the paragraph. Use the words in the Word Bank
to fill in the blanks.

North America	**landforms**	**immigrants**	**urban**
location	**rural**	**country**	**suburb**

People who move to a new place to start a new life are

_____. Many of them travel from their home

_____ to live in the United States of America.
These people look at maps to help them find a

_____, or place, that is just right for them.
Maps can show them where to find mountains, lakes, or other

_____. Maps can also show them how the land
is used. Then people can make a choice. Do they want to live

in a city, or _____ area? Do they want to live

in a _____ just outside a city? Or do they

want to live in a _____ area, where there is a lot
of open land? People can choose to live in many places on the

continent of _____.

CALIFORNIA STANDARDS HSS 2.2, 2.2.2, 2.2.3, 2.2.4

Name _____ Date _____

COMPARE AND CONTRAST
Reading Social Studies

Fill in the chart to show what you have learned about geography.

Urban

many people

_____

_____

_____

_____

_____

_____

Both

_____

_____

_____

_____

_____

_____

_____

_____

Suburban

fewer people

_____

_____

_____

_____

_____

_____

Tale of a Good Citizen

Read the story about José. Underline the things he did to be a good citizen. Then answer the questions.

José decided to spend the day being a good citizen. First, he helped his younger brother brush his hair. His mother was so pleased that she put an extra snack in his lunch bag. At school, José was careful to follow the rules all day long. Then, after school, he saw his neighbor coming home from the grocery store. José helped carry her groceries. As his father tucked him into bed that night, José said, "I had a great day. Maybe tomorrow will be even better!"

1 How did José act like a responsible citizen?

_____

_____

2 How do you know José likes being a good citizen?

_____

_____

CALIFORNIA STANDARDS HSS 2.3

Name _____ Date _____

It's a Law!

Each picture shows a person obeying a law. Write that law.

1  _____
_____
_____

2  _____
_____
_____

3  _____
_____

4  _____
_____
_____

CALIFORNIA STANDARDS HSS 2.3.1

Name _____ Date _____

MAP AND GLOBE SKILLS
States and Capitals

Look at the map. Then answer the questions.

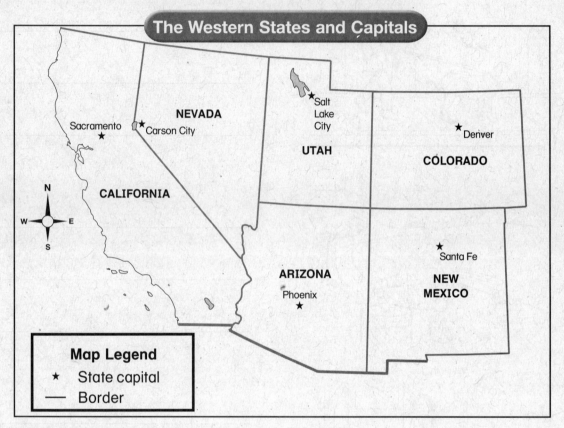

The Western States and Capitals

Salt Lake City ★

NEVADA

Sacramento ★

★ Carson City

Denver ★

UTAH

COLORADO

N
W ● E
S

CALIFORNIA

★ Santa Fe

ARIZONA
Phoenix
★

NEW MEXICO

Map Legend
★ State capital
— Border

1 What is the capital of New Mexico? _____

2 Which western states share a border with California?

_____

3 Of what state is Sacramento the capital? _____

4 Arizona shares its northern border with _____.

CALIFORNIA STANDARDS HSS 2.2; CS 4

Name _____ Date _____

Our Country's Government

Read each sentence. Fill in the blank with a word from the
Word Bank. Use each word only once.

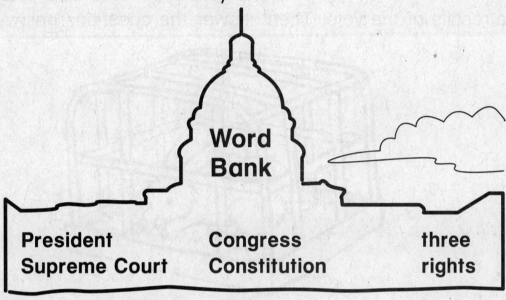

Word Bank

President   Congress   three
Supreme Court   Constitution   rights

1 Our country's government has _____ branches.

2 The written set of rules for our government is called the

_____ .

3 The _____ lives and works in the White House.

4 _____ is the branch of government that makes
the laws.

5 The _____ makes sure all laws agree with
the Constitution.

6 The Constitution says that all Americans have certain

_____ .

CALIFORNIA STANDARDS HSS 2.3, 2.3.1

Name _____ Date _____

PARTICIPATION SKILLS
Tally the Votes!

A second-grade class voted on names for the class rabbit. Look at the results of the vote. Then answer the questions below.

Names for Our Rabbit

Herman ||

Floppy ||||

Hoppy |||| |

Scooter |

① Which name got the most votes? _____

② Which name got one vote? _____

③ How many children voted? _____

CALIFORNIA STANDARDS HSS 2.3

24 ■ Homework and Practice Book Use after reading Unit 3, Skill Lesson, pages 150–151.

Name _____ Date _____

A New Nation

Make up the name of a nation where you are the leader.
Draw a flag for your nation. Then answer the questions.

1 What nation is most like your nation? Why?

_____

_____

2 What do you do as leader of your nation?

_____

_____

CALIFORNIA STANDARDS HSS 2.3, 2.3.2

Nations Around the World

Circle *yes* if the statement is true. Circle *no* if the statement is not true.

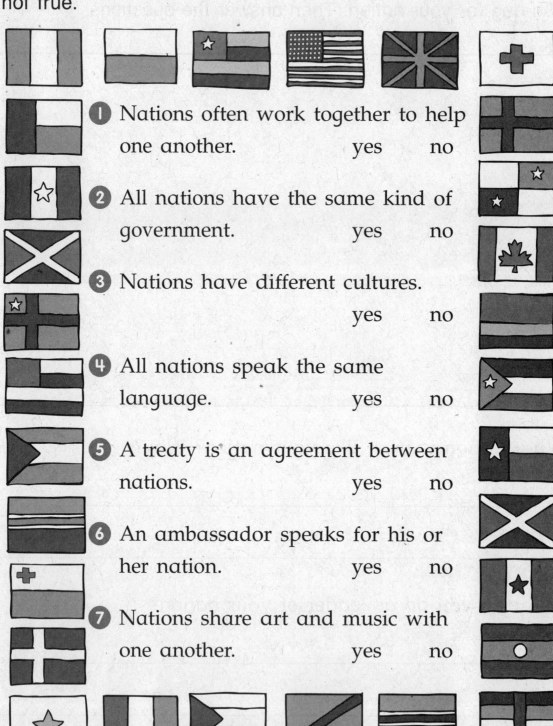

1. Nations often work together to help one another.   yes   no

2. All nations have the same kind of government.   yes   no

3. Nations have different cultures.   yes   no

4. All nations speak the same language.   yes   no

5. A treaty is an agreement between nations.   yes   no

6. An ambassador speaks for his or her nation.   yes   no

7. Nations share art and music with one another.   yes   no

CALIFORNIA STANDARDS HSS 2.3.2

26 ■ Homework and Practice Book   Use after reading Unit 3, Lesson 5, pages 158–163.

Name _____ Date _____

PARTICIPATION SKILLS
What's the Problem?

Look at the picture. Can you solve the problem?
Answer the questions below.

1 What is the problem? _____

_____

2 What caused the problem? _____

_____

3 What are some solutions to the problem? _____

_____

_____

CALIFORNIA STANDARDS HSS 2.3.2

Name _____ Date _____

Study Guide

Read the paragraph. Use the words in the Word Bank
to fill in the blanks. Use each word only once.

responsibility	President	nations	citizens
laws	mayor	governments	governor
consequences			

There are many _____, or countries, in the

world. Each one has different _____ that its

people, or _____, must follow. These rules help

keep the people in a country safe. People everywhere have

a _____ to follow the rules and to treat each

other in a fair way. People who break the rules must face

_____. They may have to pay a fine or even go

to jail. In our country, these rules are made by community,

state, and national _____. Our leaders make sure

we live in a good place. The _____ is the leader

of our community. The _____ is the leader of our

state. The _____ is the leader of our nation.

🐻 CALIFORNIA STANDARDS HSS 2.3, 2.3.1, 2.3.2

Name _____ Date _____

Fill in the chart below to show the main idea and details of this unit.

Main Idea

_____

_____

_____

Details

A government	People who	_____
makes laws	break laws	_____
that citizens	face	_____
must follow.	consequences.	_____
_____	_____	_____

Name _____ Date _____

How We Use Resources

Look at the natural resources shown in the pictures.

Write at least two ways people use each resource.

1 _____

_____

_____

2 _____

_____

_____

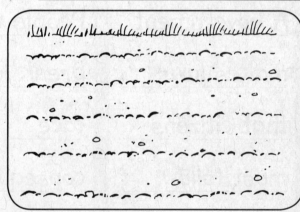

3 _____

_____

_____

4 _____

_____

_____

CALIFORNIA STANDARDS HSS 2.4.1

Name _____ Date _____

Pioneer Farmers

Draw a line to match each farmworker to the place
where he or she works on the farm.

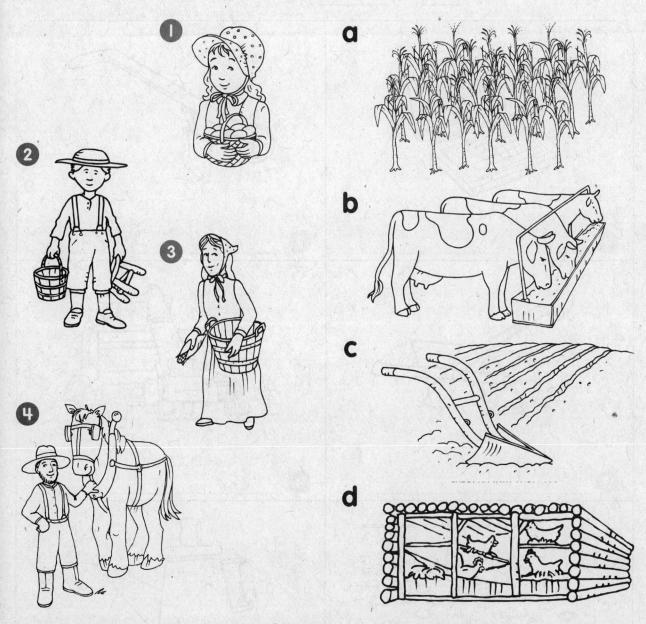

Write a sentence to tell how people got food long ago.

_____

_____

CALIFORNIA STANDARDS HSS 2.4.1

Old and New Farm Tools

Look at each picture. Does it show a farm tool from the past or the present? Write <u>past</u> or <u>present</u> on the line.

1. _____

2. _____

3. _____

4. _____

5. _____

6. _____

🐻 **CALIFORNIA STANDARDS HSS 2.4.1; CS 2**

32 ■ **Homework and Practice Book**   Use after reading Unit 4, Lesson 3, pages 202–207.

Name _____ Date _____

MAP AND GLOBE SKILLS
Make a Product Map

Create your own state. Draw an outline of your state in the box.
On the map, show the products and resources of your state.
Create a symbol for each product or resource. Make a map legend
for the symbols on your map. Write a title for your product map.

Title: _____

┌───┐
│   ┌────────────────────┐ │
│   │ Map Legend   │ │
│   │   │ │
│   │   │ │
│   │   │ │
│   │   │ │
│   │   │ │
│   │   │ │
│   │   │ │
│   │   │ │
│   └────────────────────┘ │
└───┘

What are some jobs that people do in the state you created?

_____

_____

CALIFORNIA STANDARDS HSS 2.2.2; CS 4

Processing Tomatoes

Complete the steps. Add words or pictures to show how
fresh tomatoes become canned tomatoes.

Step 1:

A farmer grows tomatoes.

Step 2:

_____

_____

_____

Step 3:

A worker sorts the
tomatoes by size.

Step 4:

A worker packs
canned tomatoes
into boxes.

Step 5:

_____

_____

🐻 CALIFORNIA STANDARDS HSS 2.4.1

34 ▪ Homework and Practice Book   Use after reading Unit 4, Lesson 4, pages 212–217.

CHART AND GRAPH SKILLS

From Beehive to Breakfast Table

Write sentences to tell what is happening in the steps. The first one is done for you.

Bees make honey.

_____

_____

_____

_____

_____

_____

_____

CALIFORNIA STANDARDS HSS 2.4.1

Name _____ Date _____

Study Guide

Read the paragraphs. Use the words in the Word Bank
to fill in the blanks.

distributor	raw materials	crops	natural resources
technology	climate	market	

Air, water, and soil are examples of _____.
Farmers have always used all of these resources to grow food.
Long ago, farmers had to worry about insects that could

harm their plants, or _____. They also

worried about bad weather. Crops need a good

_____ to grow. Today's farmers use

_____ to help them grow their crops.
    Processing plants use technology to turn

_____ into food products. Then a

_____ brings the food product from

the processing plant to the _____, or store.
This makes it possible for farmers to get their food into homes
around the world.

CALIFORNIA STANDARDS HSS 2.4, 2.4.1, 2.4.3

Name _____ Date _____

CAUSE AND EFFECT
Reading Social Studies

Use the chart to show causes and effects about our natural resources.

Cause	Effect
Plenty of rain	Crops grow

Cause	Effect
	Crops dry out

Cause	Effect

🐻 CALIFORNIA STANDARDS HSS 2.4, 2.4.1; ELA 2.2.5

Name _____ Date _____

Producers and Consumers

In each row, draw a picture to show what happens next.
Then write P under the pictures of producers and C
under the pictures of consumers.

CALIFORNIA STANDARDS HSS 2.4, 2.4.2

38 ▪ **Homework and Practice Book** Use after reading Unit 5, Lesson 1, pages 246–251.

Name _____ Date _____

CHART AND GRAPH SKILLS
Pet Sitting

This bar graph shows how many hours the pet sitter works
each day. Use the graph to answer the questions.

Pet Sitter's Hours

Monday						
Tuesday						
Wednesday						
Thursday						
Friday						

     0   1   2   3   4   5   6

1 How many hours does the pet sitter work on Tuesday? _____

2 On which day does the pet sitter work the most hours?

_____

3 On which days does the pet sitter work the same number

of hours? _____

4 On which day do you think the pet sitter sees the fewest

pets? Why? _____

_____

CALIFORNIA STANDARDS HSS 2.4.2

Name _____ Date _____

Saving, Sharing, Spending

This week you earned $10 for watering a neighbor's lawn and walking his dog. Your grandmother gave you $20 for your birthday. Answer the question. Then fill in the table.

How much money do you have in all? _____

What I Will Save	What I Will Share	What I Will Spend
• I will save _____.	• I will share _____.	• I will spend _____.
• I will put the money	• I will share the money with	• I will spend the money on
_____	_____	_____
_____	_____	_____
_____ .	_____ .	_____ .

Name _____ Date _____

CHART AND GRAPH SKILLS
Classroom Picture Graph

How many of these things are in your classroom? Use a
picture symbol to show how many of each you see.

▦	
⬗	
ABC	
📚	
🪑	

CALIFORNIA STANDARDS HSS 2.4.2

A Lot or a Little

Draw a picture to show what could happen to make the oranges scarce. Write a sentence about your picture. Then answer the question.

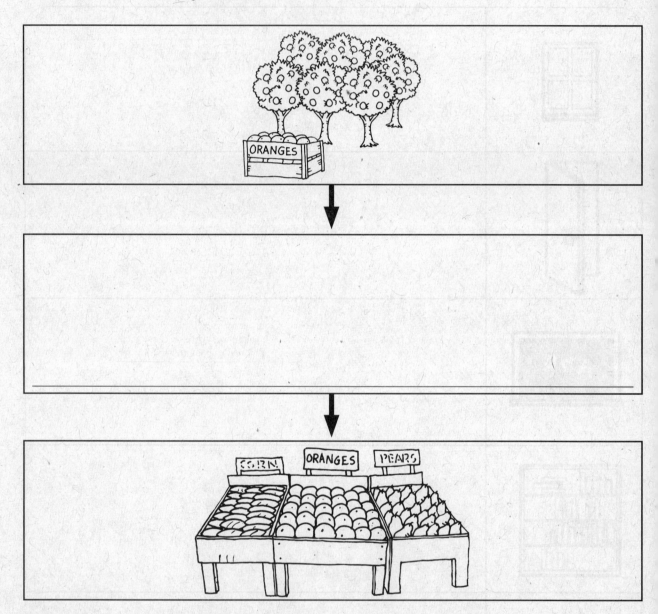

What will happen to the price of oranges if they become scarce?

_____

🐻 CALIFORNIA STANDARDS HSS 2.4, 2.4.3

42 ■ Homework and Practice Book Use after reading Unit 5, Lesson 3, pages 268–271.

Name _____ Date _____

CRITICAL THINKING SKILLS

Make Choices When Buying

The products in each row cost about the same.
Suppose that you can buy only one. Circle the
product in each row that you would buy and tell why.

1 I would buy _____
because

_____

_____.

2 I would buy _____
because

_____

_____.

3 I would buy _____
because

_____

_____.

CALIFORNIA STANDARDS HSS 2.4

Partners in Trade

The map shows three countries and some products
they trade. Use the map to answer the questions.

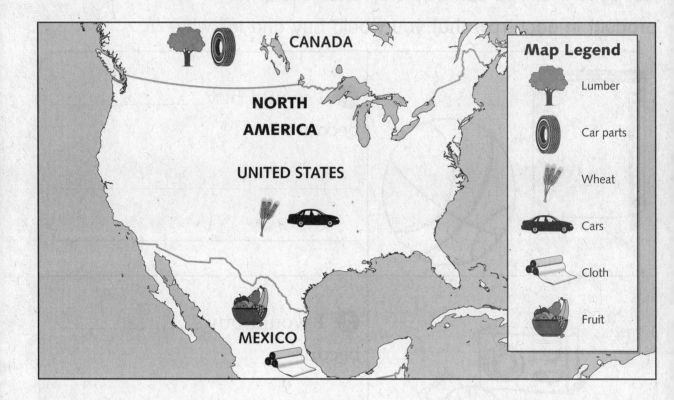

1 Henry, in the United States, loves bananas. From which

   country do bananas come? _____

2 Jamie's mother, in Canada, wants to buy a car.

   From where might her new car come? _____

3 Carlos, in Mexico, wants to build a house. From which

   country might the lumber come? _____

CALIFORNIA STANDARDS HSS 2.3.2

44 ■ Homework and Practice Book Use after reading Unit 5, Lesson 4, pages 276–279.

Name _____ Date _____

Study Guide

Read the paragraph. Use the words in the Word Bank
to fill in the blanks.

marketplace	occupation	consumers	goods
producers	factory	services	income	trade

People work at a job, or _____, so

they can earn _____ to buy things. Some

people make _____, or products that can

be bought and sold. They might work in a building called a

_____. Other people, such as dentists and

doctors, provide _____. Both types of

workers are called _____. They sell their

goods or services to _____. People go to

the _____ to find stores that sell things

that they want and need. There, people _____

money for goods or services they want.

CALIFORNIA STANDARDS HSS 2.3.2, 2.4, 2.4.2, 2.4.3

Name _____ Date _____

CATEGORIZE AND CLASSIFY
Reading Social Studies

Fill in the chart to categorize and classify information
from the unit.

Goods

Flowers
_____
_____
_____
_____

Topic

Producers
_____
_____
_____
_____
_____
_____
_____
_____
_____
_____
_____
_____
_____

Services

Health care
_____
_____
_____
_____

Occupations

Park ranger
_____
_____
_____
_____

Jobs for Children

Selling crafts
_____
_____
_____
_____

CALIFORNIA STANDARDS HSS 2.4, 2.4.2; ELA 2.2.5

Name _____ Date _____

My Hero

Complete the paragraph, and design a medal
to honor the person.

If I could choose a special person to honor, I would choose

_____. This

person is my _____. I would choose this person because

_____.

We could honor this hero by _____

_____.

Design a medal for your hero.

Name _____ Date _____

CHART AND GRAPH SKILLS
Read a Table

Look at the table, and answer the questions.

Inventions			
Transportation			
Communication			
Recreation			

1 Draw a line under the title of this table.

2 What three types of inventions are shown? _____

_____

3 Name one invention in communication. _____

_____

4 Which recreation invention could also be a transportation

invention? _____

🐻 CALIFORNIA STANDARDS HSS 2.5

Acts of Courage

Match the hero to his acts of courage. Write the letter
next to his name on the lines. You will write each
letter twice.

a. Abraham Lincoln   b. Sitting Bull

c. Jackie Robinson   d. Dr. Martin Luther King, Jr.

1 _____ He worked to end slavery.

2 _____ He was the first African American to play
professional baseball.

3 _____ He won the Nobel Peace Prize for helping people
work together.

4 _____ He was an American Indian leader.

5 _____ He led his people to fight for their land.

6 _____ He was the President of the United States of
America.

7 _____ He was a minister who talked about peace.

8 _____ He played baseball well even when people made
fun of him.

CRITICAL THINKING SKILLS
Nonfiction Books

Read the book titles. Write the titles of the nonfiction books on the book covers.

Facts About the Presidents   Abe Goes to School

The Indian and the Soldier   The True Life of Sitting Bull

Jackie Strikes Out   Jackie Robinson, A Biography

CALIFORNIA STANDARDS HSS 2.5; HR 3

Name _____   Date _____

Volunteers Wanted!

Match each volunteer with a volunteer job. Draw a line
from the person on the left to the job on the right.

1 Ana likes animals.

ELMWOOD HOSPITAL NEEDS VOLUNTEERS TO VISIT CHILDREN IN THE HOSPITAL.

2 Ben enjoys cooking.

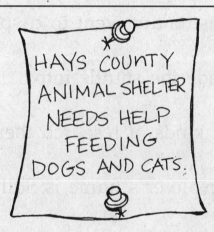

HAYS COUNTY ANIMAL SHELTER NEEDS HELP FEEDING DOGS AND CATS.

3 Nhan makes balloon toys.

VOLUNTEERS NEEDED TO HELP PREPARE HOT MEALS.

CALIFORNIA STANDARDS HSS 2.5

Name _____ Date _____

Explorer Poem

Write a word on each line to complete the poem.

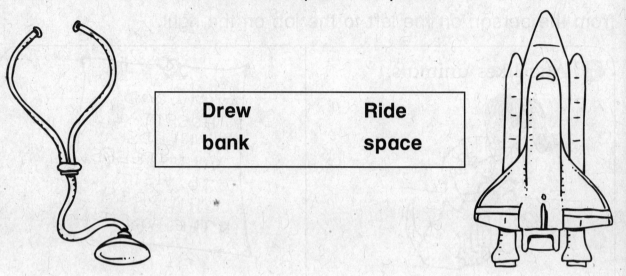

Drew	Ride
bank	space

This astronaut went to a special place.

She rode the shuttle into _____.

Many kinds of research there she tried.

This explorer's name is Sally _____.

Another explorer we all can thank

Found a way to store blood in a _____.

This great discovery saves lives. It's true!

This explorer's name is Dr. Charles _____.

CALIFORNIA STANDARDS HSS 2.5

52 ▪ **Homework and Practice Book** Use after reading Unit 6, Lesson 4, pages 322–325.

Name _____ Date _____

Study Guide

Read the paragraph. Use the words in the Word Bank
to fill in the blanks.

compassion	invention	scientist	courage
explorer	hero	inventor	

A _____ is a person who has done something

brave or important. Thomas Edison was an _____.

His _____ of the electric lightbulb changed the lives
of people forever. George Washington Carver was a

_____ who taught farmers how to make soil

good for growing their crops. It took _____,
or bravery, for Sitting Bull to lead his people to fight for their

land. Another brave person is an _____ named
Sally Ride. She studied new things in space. Not many people

have as much _____ as Mother Teresa did. She
spent her life caring for others. The world is a better place
because of these heroes.

RECALL AND RETELL

Reading Social Studies

Use the chart to recall and retell details about people who make a difference in others' lives.

Recall Detail

Scientists observe things and make discoveries.

Retell

_____
_____
_____
_____
_____
_____
_____
_____
_____
_____
_____
_____
_____
_____
_____
_____

Recall Detail

_____
_____
_____

Recall Detail

_____
_____
_____

 CALIFORNIA STANDARDS HSS 2.5; ELA 2.2.5